THE FIRST BOOK OF
AUTOMOBILES

Franklin Watts, Inc.
845 Third Avenue
New York, N.Y. 10022

THE FIRST BOOK OF
AUTOMOBILES

Second Revised Edition

written and illustrated by

JEANNE BENDICK

The author's thanks to Robert Bendick, for the
revision of this book; to Carl H. Turnquist,
of the Cass Technical High School in Detroit,
Michigan; to Dave Garroway; to Robin
McGuire, for his special assistance; and
to the many other automobile and accessory
people who helped with this book.

CONTENTS

HOW MANY KINDS OF AUTOMOBILES?

If you stand on a busy street corner, you will see dozens of kinds of automobiles in no time at all: family cars, buses and trucks, fire engines, tow trucks, snowplows or street cleaners, trailers, campers, dump trucks, tank trucks, sports cars, and maybe even some cars with electric motors.

6

An automobile moves by itself. (This is what the word "automobile" means.) An automobile carries its own power. It does not have to be pushed or pulled unless its power is out of order.

To build an automobile and keep it going takes many different kinds of products. It takes steel, rubber and glass, plastics and leather, cotton, porcelain and chrome, paint, gasoline, oil and grease, water, wool, chemicals, and lots more.

Some cars are so small that only two people can fit into them. Some buses are so big that they can carry almost a hundred passengers. Some cars have clear tops through which you can see the sky. Some have no tops at all. Some motors are in the front; some are in the back. Some are in the middle. But in many important ways cars are alike.

7

CARS FOR FAMILIES

Most of the automobiles you see are stock cars—general-purpose cars that are not built to special order. Many family cars are sedans. A sedan has a front seat and a back seat and holds five or six people. Some sedans have four doors and some have only two. A very small family might have a car with no back seat at all.

If your family likes sports, you may have some sort of special rack that fastens to the top of your car. You may carry skis there, or fishing rods, or even a canoe. Some cars have racks in back, fastened to the trunk.

Some people have convertibles. They can make an open car out of a closed one any time they want to.

Big families or families who are always carrying things often have station wagons. A station wagon is part sedan, part truck. Some station wagons have three rows of seats. When all the seats are in, nine people can ride comfortably. Two rows of seats fold down, making plenty of room for baggage, or for children to play or sleep. Two or three large dogs can ride there, and a family can even carry a rowboat.

A station wagon has the same kind of wheels and bottom that a sedan has, but the car body is different. The space that is the trunk in a sedan is used to make the extra room inside a station wagon.

Some station wagons look more like buses. They are high and have extra doors that open on the sides. There is a lot of room inside—even more than in a regular station wagon. People can sit all the way up front because the engine is under the floor in back. There is even room for a pony to ride inside.

Families who like to camp often have buses like this equipped for camping. They have bunks and sometimes a place to cook and even a chemical toilet.

Some families have campers that fit onto pickup trucks. When the families are not camping, they use the truck for ordinary driving.

Many house trailers hitch on to cars. Some trailers are plain and some are fancy. Most of them have bunks or

beds to sleep in, a little kitchen with a stove and an icebox, a bathroom with a shower, cupboards for dishes, and closets for clothes. Fancy trailers have telephones, air conditioners, and television sets. Some trailers are so big that they have to be moved by trucks.

If you travel in a trailer you might stay in a trailer park with lots of other trailers. The trailers are put in rows like the houses on a street. There will probably be a water connection, a place to plug in and get electricity, a laundry where you can do your wash, a restaurant, and even an open-air movie.

Some trailers are not for living in, but are big enough to carry a great deal of luggage or to take a horse or two to a horse show, or a boat to the nearest lake or ocean.

CARS FOR ROUGH DRIVING

Some cars are specially made for rough, hard driving in sand or snow or mud and even where there are no roads. They are more ruggedly built than ordinary cars, with stiffer springs and less fancy bodies. They have four-wheel drive and extra-low gears (see page 24) that can give less speed and more power when it is needed.

Most family cars have no power to the front wheels. A car with four-wheel drive has a drive shaft to the front wheels. This shaft gives the front wheels power to pull the car through rough places while the rear wheels push it. Jeeps, Scouts, Land Rovers, and Land Cruisers have this kind of power.

FERRARI

ROLLS-ROYCE

FOREIGN CARS

More automobiles are made in the United States than anywhere else, but many other countries build good cars. Many foreign cars are small, with fewer cylinders and less horsepower (see page 14). They are designed to use less gasoline. Small cars make good sense in most foreign countries. Gasoline is very expensive, people drive shorter distances, and many roads are old and narrow.

If you look around, you will see small cars that were made in Japan, Italy, Sweden, France, England, and maybe other countries.

One of the most popular cars all over the world is the German Volkswagen. Its motor is in the rear and the luggage is stored in front, under the hood.

VOLKSWAGEN

JAGUAR

RENAULT

SPORTS CARS

Sports cars are not really family cars unless the family is very small, because there is hardly ever room for more than two people and maybe a dog. Most sports cars have bucket seats, one for each passenger. Sports cars look like racing automobiles, and many are used for racing.

The HORSEPOWER of many sports cars is less than that of most family cars. Horsepower is the measurement of power in an engine. Long ago, James Watt figured out that a horse could lift a weight of 550 pounds one foot off the ground in one second, and that is called one horsepower. Family cars usually have horsepower of 180 to 350. Many sports cars have engines of under 160 horsepower.

1 HORSEPOWER

Sports cars can go as fast or faster than cars with more horsepower because they use different combinations of gears. (See page 24.)

You have to shift the gears of most sports cars. They do not have automatic shifts.

Sports cars are built closer to the ground than ordinary sedans are, and their bodies are fastened to the wheels with different kinds of springs and bars. This build makes the whole car hug the road better, even around curves.

RACING CARS AND RACES

A real racing car cannot be used for anything else. It was built just for racing. Some racing cars do not even have a starter, because all the unnecessary weight and moving parts have been removed. On a track, racing automobiles are pulled or pushed to start.

Racing cars have a crew: the driver and one or more mechanics who do a fast fixing job if anything goes wrong during the race. The smallest racing cars are the midgets, which look almost like toys and can race in a ball park or even inside a building.

A lot of automobile racing is done in sports cars and stock cars. Today's stock cars go faster than the racing cars of thirty years ago, and the ordinary gasoline they use now is better than the racing gasoline used to be.

Some people who enjoy driving fast like to race their cars, and there are special tracks and special races just for them. Some communities have drag strips, where older teenagers can race their cars under supervision.

There are several famous automobile races held every year. One is a race held every Memorial Day in Indianapolis, Indiana. The cars race 500 miles around a track that was originally built as a testing place for automobile manufacturers' cars.

Another race is the Grand Prix, a road race that goes through the Alps and across France, through villages and towns, while people cheer and wave from their windows.

The most powerful racing cars built do not race against each other. They race against time. They go so fast and are so big that there is not room for them on any track in the world. Some race across the salt flats at Bonneville, Utah, or across the sand at Daytona Beach in Florida. One car has been timed at more than 600 miles an hour. One special racing car has a 17,000-horsepower jet engine.

HOW AUTOMOBILES WORK

An automobile has about seven thousand different parts in it.

These are the important working sections of a car:
the ENGINE,
the FUEL SYSTEM,
the ALTERNATOR,
the TRANSMISSION SYSTEM,
the COOLING SYSTEM,
the CLUTCH or AUTOMATIC TRANSMISSION,
the DIFFERENTIAL,
the STEERING SYSTEM,
the WHEELS and BRAKES.

Everything is attached to the FRAME. When all the parts (except the body) are in place, they are called the CHASSIS (pronounced SHAS-ee).

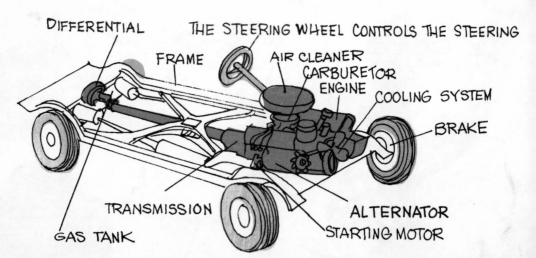

DIFFERENTIAL
THE STEERING WHEEL CONTROLS THE STEERING
FRAME
AIR CLEANER
CARBURETOR
ENGINE
COOLING SYSTEM
BRAKE
TRANSMISSION
GAS TANK
ALTERNATOR
STARTING MOTOR

The first thing a driver does to start the car is put his key into the IGNITION LOCK and turn the key. The key opens a path so that electric current can flow from the car BATTERY to the SPARK PLUGS. When the key is turned farther, it starts the STARTER MOTOR, which is just powerful enough to make the engine begin turning.

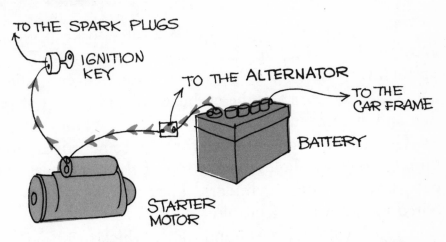

TO THE SPARK PLUGS

IGNITION KEY

TO THE ALTERNATOR

TO THE CAR FRAME

BATTERY

STARTER MOTOR

The starter gets its electricity from the STORAGE BATTERY, which does all the electrical jobs in your car. It starts the car, runs the radio, the heater, the windshield wipers, the horn, and the lights. If electricity kept flowing out of the battery and none ever came in, soon it would all be used up. The battery would be dead. So the battery is attached to the ALTERNATOR. The alternator's job is to make electricity from the car's engine power when it is running, and send the electricity back to the battery to replace the current that has been used.

19

When the starter motor turns the engine over, the gasoline pump starts pumping gas from the tank into the CARBURETOR. The carburetor looks like this.

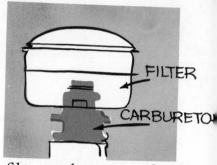

FILTER

CARBURETOR

The big round thing on top is a filter to keep out dust and dirt. The carburetor is a mixer. It mixes gasoline from the tank with air — 2,000 gallons of air with every gallon of gas. What comes out of the carburetor is a fine fog of gasoline and air, mixed.

This gasoline fog is forced through some valves (which are little one-way holes) to the top of the CYLINDERS. Most cars have 4, 6, or 8 cylinders. They are can-shaped holes bored into a heavy metal block.

In each cylinder is a round slice of thick metal on a rod. This is called the PISTON. The piston moves up and down in the cylinder. At the top of each cylinder there is a SPARK PLUG.

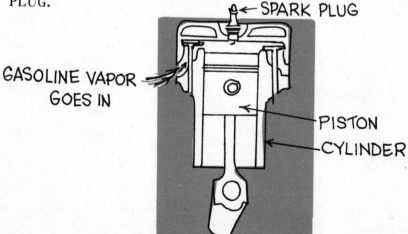

← SPARK PLUG

GASOLINE VAPOR GOES IN

PISTON

CYLINDER

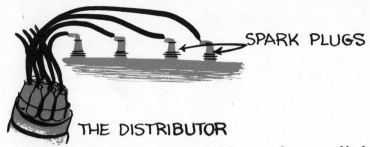

SPARK PLUGS

THE DISTRIBUTOR

Every spark plug is connected by a wire to a little round box called the DISTRIBUTOR. The distributor hands out electricity to the spark plugs, one after the other, very fast, thousands of sparks a minute.

At the end of each spark plug there are two heavy wires with a space between them. When the current jumps across the space, it makes a hot spark that sets fire to the gasoline vapor all around it.

BANG! There is an explosion in the cylinder.

SPARK JUMPS ACROSS SPACE

The explosion pushes the piston down.

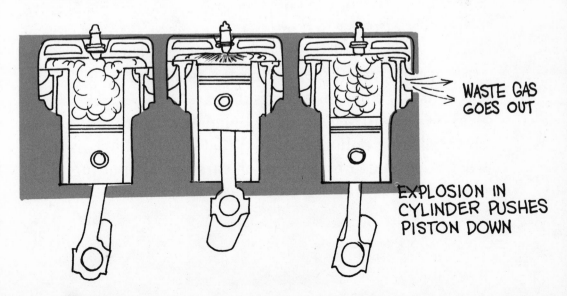

WASTE GAS GOES OUT

EXPLOSION IN CYLINDER PUSHES PISTON DOWN

The piston is attached to a rod.

The rod is attached to the CRANKSHAFT of the car.

As the rods are pushed down, one after the other, they push the crankshaft around, just the way your foot (attached to your pushing leg) pushes the pedal of your bicycle around.

The crankshaft turns the TRANSMISSION GEARS, which turn the DRIVE SHAFT, which turns the DIFFERENTIAL, which turns the rear axle, which turns the rear wheels.

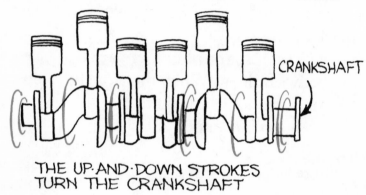

CRANKSHAFT

THE UP-AND-DOWN STROKES
TURN THE CRANKSHAFT

In older cars, after each explosion in the cylinder, the waste or partly burned-up gas goes out through a valve, through a MUFFLER that muffles the explosions in the engine, and into a pipe called the EXHAUST. The exhaust shoots the waste gas out behind the car. In cars made now, partly burned gas is recycled before it leaves the car.

This exhaust gas is a combination of dirty, dangerous chemicals that pollute the air. What do you think happens when thousands or millions of cars are all putting these chemicals into the air we breathe?

Now that the car is running, the cooling system is at work. The engine gets very hot with all those explosions taking place in it. If it were not being cooled all the time, the parts would crack or melt together.

The FAN sucks air in through the front of the car to cool the water in the car RADIATOR. This water then flows back through the WATER JACKET around the engine cylinders, to cool them off.

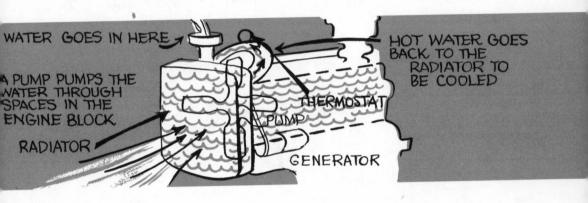

WATER GOES IN HERE

A PUMP PUMPS THE
WATER THROUGH
SPACES IN THE
ENGINE BLOCK

RADIATOR

THERMOSTAT

PUMP

GENERATOR

HOT WATER GOES
BACK TO THE
RADIATOR TO
BE COOLED

If the temperature outside is below freezing, antifreeze must be added to the water in a water-cooled engine to keep it from freezing when the car is not running.

Some engines are designed in a different way. They are cooled by air only.

While a car is running, oil is pumped all through the engine to keep the moving parts sliding smoothly past one another.

23

Now the engine is running smoothly and you want to get moving. The gears in the transmission start the work of carrying the power to the wheels. There are at least three sets of gears in the transmissions of most passenger cars, and even more in jeeps, trucks, and some foreign cars.

Gears can do three things. They can change the speed or power or direction of a force.

The transmission changes a little "twist" or "torque" (pronounced TORK), which is turning-power, into a lot of torque.

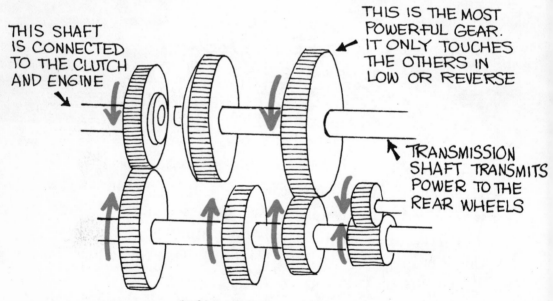

THIS SHAFT IS CONNECTED TO THE CLUTCH AND ENGINE

THIS IS THE MOST POWERFUL GEAR. IT ONLY TOUCHES THE OTHERS IN LOW OR REVERSE

TRANSMISSION SHAFT TRANSMITS POWER TO THE REAR WHEELS

LOW GEAR
THE GEARS CHANGE POSITION WITH EACH SPEED

The first set of gears has the hardest work of all — to start the car moving. Things that are standing still are hard to start. When the next set of gears is used, the car picks up speed. Finally, when the car is moving easily, the gears are shifted again. We say then that the car is in high gear.

Unless it has an automatic transmission to shift the gears, every car has a CLUTCH, which takes the pressure off the gears so that they can shift. The driver has to step on a pedal to release the clutch, then shift the gears with a lever.

When the driver wants to go backward, the gears work like the powerful low gear, but in the opposite direction.

The gears in the transmission multiply the torque or speed from the engine, and send it back to the rear axle by way of the drive shaft. On most cars, the rear wheels of the car push it ahead. The front wheels only steer.

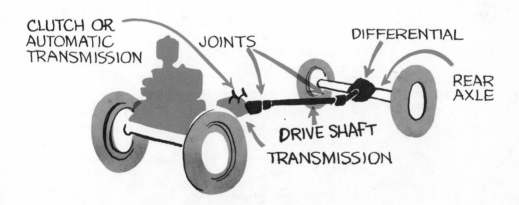

CLUTCH OR
AUTOMATIC
TRANSMISSION

JOINTS

DIFFERENTIAL

REAR
AXLE

DRIVE SHAFT

TRANSMISSION

The drive shaft has joints, just as your arms and legs have. The joints allow the shaft to move up and down as the wheels go over bumps. Where the drive shaft meets the rear axle (which is a rod connecting the back wheels), there is the group of gears called the differential.

These gears turn the rear wheels. They let each wheel turn at its own speed when it is necessary. If the car is turning a corner, the outside wheel has to turn faster than the inside one, which acts as a sort of pivot.

Another set of gears connects the STEERING WHEEL to the front wheels that steer the car.

The FOOT BRAKE pedal and the PARKING BRAKE are connected to the wheels. When you press on the foot brake, friction "shoes" push hard against the rim of the wheel drums to stop the wheels from turning.

Another kind of brake is the DISK BRAKE. Two pads push against a disk on each wheel and stop the wheels.

The parking brake is connected only to the rear wheels.

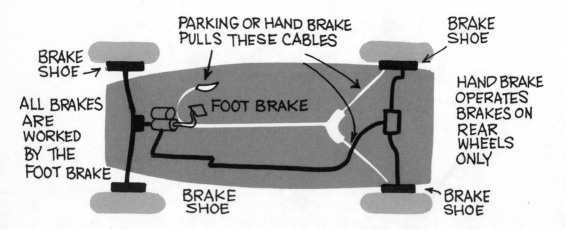

PARKING OR HAND BRAKE PULLS THESE CABLES

BRAKE SHOE

BRAKE SHOE →

ALL BRAKES ARE WORKED BY THE FOOT BRAKE

FOOT BRAKE

HAND BRAKE OPERATES BRAKES ON REAR WHEELS ONLY

BRAKE SHOE

BRAKE SHOE

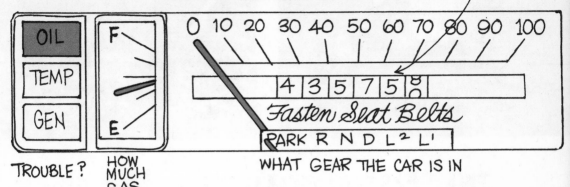

HOW FAST THE CAR IS GOING   HOW FAR IT HAS GONE

OIL   TEMP   GEN   F   E

0 10 20 30 40 50 60 70 80 90 100

4 3 5 7 5 | 8/0

Fasten Seat Belts

PARK R N D L² L¹

TROUBLE?   HOW MUCH GAS   WHAT GEAR THE CAR IS IN

You can read many kinds of information on the DASH-BOARD of a car.

There are dials that show how much gas is in the tank, how fast the car is going, and how far it has gone.

In some cars, dials show what the oil pressure and the engine temperature are, and whether the electrical system is working right.

In other cars there are no dials. But lights go on if anything is wrong in these systems.

Some sports cars have an instrument that shows how fast the engine is turning. Some cars have a CHOKE on the instrument panel. Pulling out the choke keeps some of the air from going into the carburetor, so there is more gasoline and less air. That gives the car extra power. All cars have chokes, but most of them are automatic.

THE CHOKE IS JUST A LITTLE KNOB ON THE INSTRUMENT PANEL

ENGLISH STEAM CARRIAGE

DAIMLER'S MOTOR CARRIAGE

THE FIRST AUTOMOBILES

For many hundreds of years before automobiles were invented, men dreamed and worked over the idea of building a machine that could travel freely under its own power. The first ancestor of today's cars was built in France before the American Revolution. It was a steam tractor that almost scared the French farmers out of their wits as it puffed and smoked down the roads.

The English were working with steam power too, and by the beginning of the nineteenth century they had built so many steam carriages that a law was passed saying that every steam carriage on the road had to have a man walking in front with a red flag or a lantern to warn of danger.

In the years that followed, most horseless-carriage inventors worked with steam engines. Others experimented with electric motors and the newly developed gasoline engine. In 1887, a German named Gottlieb Daimler put a one-cylinder motor on his carriage, left his horse in the barn, and went out driving. Another inventor, Charles Benz, put

28

MOTOR
TRICYCLE

DURYEA'S MOTOR
ROAD WAGON

his gasoline engine on a tricycle.

But an inventor in Paris decided that these new engines should have a vehicle designed especially for them. Levassor built the first real automobile in 1892. It had a special place for the motor and even had a clutch and gears.

American inventors began experimenting and building autos, too. Cars were built with steam, electric, and gasoline engines, and everyone argued over which was best. On Thanksgiving Day in 1895 there was a 92-mile race through the streets of Chicago for a $5,000 prize. An American car built by Charles Duryea was the only one that finished the course. It had a gasoline motor.

Many inventors and manufacturers started building automobiles. At first the cars were so expensive that only very rich people could afford them. Ransom Olds, who started the Oldsmobile factory, built the first low-priced car, but it was Henry Ford who put cars into mass production. Now many, many millions of families own automobiles.

SOME FAMOUS EARLY CARS

Here are some of the most famous early automobiles. Some of these models are still running today.

This is the first motor vehicle, built in France by Captain Cugnot in 1769. It ran by steam power.

In 1898, Alexander Winton built the first delivery truck.

A Model T Ford, 1910.

This Knox, built in 1900, was like a giant tricycle.

In 1904, this was an Oldsmobile Sports Car!

The Electric Brougham (pronounced BROOM) looked exactly like an old coach without horses.

This is a White Steamer, built in 1900.

The Mercer Raceabout, 1911, was one of the greatest American sports cars ever built. Some are still in use.

In 1909, Packard came out with a hard-top car. If you wanted the sun you could ride in the back, which was convertible.

CARS HAVE CHANGED AMERICA

Before so many people had automobiles, America's whole way of living was different.

If you wanted to take a long journey, you went by train. You would take a short trip in a horse and carriage.

If you lived outside a town or on a farm, you might go once a week or even every other week to shop for groceries. The trip would take a long time, usually a whole day. Farmers depended on their horses for plowing, for delivering fruit and vegetables, for hauling grain, for carting cans of milk. Most goods were carried by rail or boat.

In cities, horses pulled delivery wagons and even the trolley cars that most people took uptown and down. Some families owned a horse and buggy or had a team of matched horses to pull their carriage.

Automobiles changed everything.

Nowadays you can live in the country and drive to the city to work every day. If you live in the city, you can drive out to the country to spend a day and be back in time for supper. You can drive over a hundred miles to see your grandmother and come home the same day. You can spend an evening with friends several towns away.

Fifty years ago, most people seldom traveled more than a few miles away from where they lived. Now whole families get in their cars and go across the country to see the sights. Families from New England travel down to Florida. Families from Los Angeles can drive away from the palm trees, up to the mountains for a day's skiing. Canadians visit the United States for a few hours' shopping. Americans go to Mexico.

DAY'S JOURNEY NOW COULD TAKE YOU TO ANOTHER CLIMATE

Before there were trucks and automobiles, it was very hard for a family to move. They had to take all their possessions by wagon, or ship them by train or boat. Most people stayed where they had always lived.

Now, great numbers of people move from one part of the country to another. They go where the jobs are, or to a climate they like better. Many families live in mobile homes. These houses on wheels can be moved to a new place at any time.

Most products are moved by truck. Trucks carry goods from city to city, from door to door, wherever there is a road.

Automobiles have made millions of jobs. People build cars and fix them, sell gas, build and maintain roads. Other people work in industries that supply materials to make cars.

But automobiles have changed America in less helpful ways, too. Automobiles have made big problems.

More and more roads are built, paving over fields and forests. Towns and cities sprawl out along the roads, taking over still more of the countryside. There are so many cars in cities that getting from one part of a city to another is hard and slow. Gasoline fumes pollute the air in every city.

Because there are so many cars, hundreds of thousands of people are killed or hurt in automobile accidents every year.

Worn-out cars are hard to get rid of. Nobody wants them. They clutter city streets and country roads. They make huge junk piles.

Unless people solve these problems, what is harmful about automobiles is going to be more important than what is good.

NEW CITIES HAVE WIDE STREETS AND PLENTY OF PARKING ROOM.

CARS WITH JOBS

As new cities grow up they are planned with very wide streets that will carry lots of traffic, and with parking places to hold great numbers of cars.

But if you live in a city that grew up before automobiles were invented, the streets are narrow and there are not many places to park. Unless they travel underground, in subways, many people get around in taxicabs and buses.

Most taxis are sedans. In big cities, taxis keep moving through the streets. When you need a cab, you can hail one. In some other places, taxis have two-way radios. When you phone the taxi office for a cab, the dispatcher calls the drivers on the radio and tells the one nearest your house to pick you up.

OLD CITIES HAVE CROWDED STREETS AND NO ROOM FOR PARKING.

Where lots of people travel in the same direction, buses are convenient and cheaper than taxis. Most towns and all cities have bus lines.

Many buses travel between cities. These buses are big and fast. Often people take long trips by bus. Buses built for traveling are very comfortable. The seats are up high so that you can see the countryside easily, and baggage is stored in a compartment at the bottom. Most cross-country buses have air conditioning, and observation domes made out of glass so that you can see the tops of mountains and the stars at night. Some even have bathrooms.

HELP!

Whenever you need help, it is fairly certain that some kind of automobile will come to the rescue.

Your doctor comes in a car with special license plates that tell the police what he is. In some states, registered nurses have special license plates too, with the letters RN on them. When you see a license that says RX, the car probably belongs to a druggist. DDS means a dentist.

If you phone the police, the man at the police station looks at a map that shows him where all the patrol cars are. He calls the car closest to you on the two-way radio. That patrol car may answer your call in less than a minute.

Big-city police departments have trucks that carry many different kinds of emergency equipment. If there is a sudden, heavy storm they even deliver raincoats and boots to traffic policemen on duty.

HOOK AND LADDER TRUCK

HOSE WAGON

Fire engines come in all shapes and sizes, from the chief's car — which is a red sedan with a bell, a siren, and a two-way radio for ordering more fire engines — to the hook-and-ladder truck, which is an automobile so long that a second driver has to operate the rear wheels. Between these two in size are searchlight trucks, pumpers, hose trucks, and even a canteen truck to make hot coffee and sandwiches for the firemen.

When an ambulance comes to the rescue, it rides on extra springs so that the patient won't bounce, even if the road is rough. A special bed can be wheeled in and out through the wide back doors, and there are all kinds of equipment for the ambulance doctor to use. There is usually an extra chair inside so that someone can sit with the patient.

AMBULANCE

TRUCKS ARE AUTOMOBILES

Trucks are automobiles built to do big jobs. Usually they have more gear shifts, bigger brakes, and often more wheels than ordinary cars. Some even have a different kind of engine — a DIESEL.

You can usually tell a diesel by the smokestack that carries its exhaust up into the air.

Diesel engines are different from gasoline engines.

They burn special oil instead of gasoline.

They have no carburetors or spark plugs.

While automobiles have just one body, trucks often have two parts that can be unhitched. The part with the engine, where the driver sits, is called the cab or tractor. The section that carries the load is called the trailer. In some parts of the country you may see two, or even three, trailers, hitched one behind the other to a single cab.

Some trailers have a complete set of wheels. Others have only the rear wheels. Their fronts rest on the back ends of the cabs. These are called semitrailers.

Big trailer trucks look like railway boxcars, and they do the same jobs. Sometimes whole trailers are loaded onto railway flatcars. The containers of some trailers are lifted off the wheels and loaded onto ships.

DIESEL TRAILER

SEMITRAILER

HOW A DIESEL ENGINE WORKS

Air is drawn into the cylinders. The piston compresses, or squeezes, the air up toward the top until it gets very hot.

At the top of the diesel cylinder there is a fuel valve that sprays the oil in. The heat from the compressed air sets fire to the oil.

The fast-burning oil produces a lot of pressure, which pushes down the piston.

The up-and-down movement of the piston turns the crankshaft just as it does in a gasoline engine.

Valves at the top let out the waste gases, and the cylinder takes in more air for the next stroke.

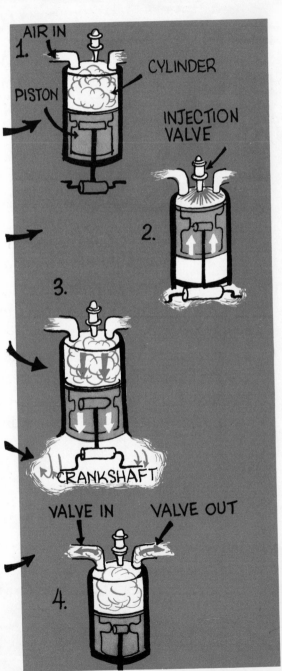

41

TRUCKS FOR DELIVERY

The main job of trucks is to pick up and deliver goods. Most trucks are specially built to do their work.

The milkman comes in a truck that is built to run very quietly and do a great deal of starting and stopping. It may even have an electric motor instead of a gas engine.

All day, trucks come and go along the main street of your town, delivering food and all the other things you need. Some bring meat, ice cream, and frozen food in giant refrigerator trucks. You can tell these by the boxlike freezing units on the front of the trailers. Frozen-food trucks are real freezers; meat trucks are not quite that cold; and garden-produce trucks are just cool. Bottled-goods trucks have racks outside. The glassman's truck has special racks too, for carrying large sheets of glass safely.

Many delivery trucks bring boxes from factories to stores. If they have heavy things to deliver, they are usually built with elevator tail hoists for lowering their loads to the ground.

Trucks that deliver dresses and suits carry them on racks so that the clothes will not get wrinkled. The racks themselves can be wheeled from place to place. The trucks that deliver things from department stores to you are sometimes powered by electric motors. (Drivers call these trucks "juice wagons" because "juice" is a slang word for electricity.) Trucks — and moving vans too — that deliver furniture are usually padded inside so that things will not get scratched.

Trucks that take money from one bank to another are armor-plated. There are no windows in the back part — just tiny portholes for the guard who sits inside to peek through.

TANKS ON WHEELS

Some trucks are great rolling tanks. Most milk companies send their milk to the bottling plants in these tank trucks, which are specially lined with layers of glass, insulation, and steel, and are refrigerated to keep the milk fresh and sweet. Every night they are cleaned with steam and scrubbing brushes.

Liquid sugar for candy factories, and syrup for soft drinks, travel by tank trucks, too. The sugar and syrup are usually pumped through big hoses from the truck to storage tanks in the cellar of the factory, or into and out of the hold of a tanker ship.

STEEL
CORK
GLASS

Oil for houses and factories, and gasoline for service stations, are tank cargo. (Tanks loaded with gasoline have big DANGER signs on their backs, because gasoline is very explosive.) Tanks haul chemicals, loads of liquid laundry bleach, vinegar, molasses, and even medicine.

A tank like the one below hauls chicken feed, which is sucked out through a pump into the farmer's bins.

BULK FEED

Some street-cleaning trucks are tanks with sprayers underneath, for washing the pavements. Other tanks carry tar, spreading it evenly on roads through nozzles in the back.

HEAVY JOBS

Some trucks are designed to do the heavy jobs. Each kind is built for its own particular work. Some have as many as ten speeds forward and three in reverse.

Some carry immense boulders or haul great logs.

Some can move a whole house from one town to another on a trailer built like this, and can set it down gently in a new place.

If someone would rather build a new house, a truck can bring a prefabricated one in a single delivery. The walls have their windows already in, the roof is in sections, and there is everything else that is needed to put the house together — even the carpenters.

An automobile delivery truck and trailer hauls new cars from the factory to the dealer, six or eight at a time. A ramp on the trailer lets down so that the cars can be driven right off into the showroom.

A hopper truck carries enormous loads of coal from the mine to the storage bins.

Long, flat gooseneck trailers are often used to carry oversized loads. They carry tractors and steam shovels to places where they are going to work. They carry large tanks and boilers to be installed in factories or on ships. Sometimes tractors with alligator trailers carry whole sections of a ship from the factory to a shipyard where they will be assembled.

Before sending one of these huge loads, someone drives over the route to see whether there are any low bridges or railway underpasses, low electric wires, or sharp and narrow turns that the load will be unable to squeeze through. If there are, the route man must try to find a road around the obstacle. If there is no other way, he must have the help of the power company, the police, or the telephone company to remove the obstacle. When finally the driver starts out, he follows a map that shows him exactly what streets and roads to take.

THE FIXING TRUCKS

Most of the fixing trucks you see are the automobile fixers themselves: the tow and service trucks. They carry jacks for raising a car so that a repairman can change a tire

or get underneath the car. They carry small generators for shooting a quick charge into a battery if it needs it. And in case a car still will not start, there is a hook and a winch on the truck so the serviceman can fasten it to the car bumper and tow the car to his garage.

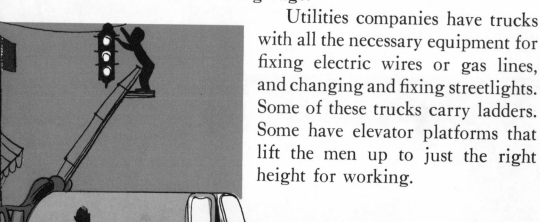

Utilities companies have trucks with all the necessary equipment for fixing electric wires or gas lines, and changing and fixing streetlights. Some of these trucks carry ladders. Some have elevator platforms that lift the men up to just the right height for working.

Telephone companies have their own repair trucks. Some are big enough to carry new telephone poles. Most of them carry tents so that the men working up on the lines can be shielded from strong winds and rain.

Some repair trucks are actually machine shops on wheels. They go to things that are too large or clumsy to bring to them. They go to farms to mend broken tractors or other farm machinery. They go to boatyards to fix boats. They have lathes and drills for making new parts, and a welding machine for putting broken parts together again.

Maybe you know a scissors grinder who comes around in a truck. He has machinery to sharpen scissors and knives and to fix broken umbrellas, garden tools, and lawn mowers.

SERVICE ON WHEELS

Many of the services and amusements people used to find only in buildings have taken to the road. This is especially handy for people who live out in the country.

Trucks have been turned into butcher shops, grocery stores, offices for keeping books or typing letters, libraries, beauty parlors, and theaters.

In some traveling puppet shows, the back of the truck becomes a stage. Inside are hooks for keeping dozens of puppets, all the props and scenery, and sometimes even folding camp chairs for the audience.

50

Groups of actors who move around the country putting on plays keep their costumes and scenery in a big trailer truck. In the summer they might even take a huge tent to use in places where there are no theaters. Sometimes whole orchestras with all their instruments (except, of course, a piano) go from town to town in their own private buses.

Bookmobiles serve people in places where regular library buildings are far apart. You can choose a book from shelves like those in any library. You have plenty of time to read your book before returning it the next time the bookmobile comes around.

Trucks carry doctors, X-ray machines, and other medical equipment to factories, to very large farms and orchards at harvesttime, and to crowded areas where there are not enough hospitals. The doctors can examine a great number of people in a short time, where they live or work.

Animal hospitals on wheels make rounds, too. When the veterinarian comes with his traveling hospital, you can bring your dog, cat, bird, or even a cow for him to see.

The United States government has highway post offices that not only carry mail between places where there is no other mail service, but also carry men to sort and cancel mail and do other post-office business on the way.

Television control rooms on wheels carry all the equipment needed for televising a program anywhere it happens to be. There are cameras and a control room, video-tape-recording equipment, a transmitter for relaying the picture, and even a generator to supply the power all that equipment needs.

There are schools on wheels. Voter-registration booths on wheels carry polling booths, so that people who have never voted before can learn how to use them. In some places there are even churches on wheels.

ODD CARS

In places where there is a lot of snow for a large part of the year, many people use skimobiles. These have skis and treads instead of wheels.

On the Sahara Desert, where there are no roads, trucks with trailers like that above carry the pipes for oil pipelines. The front and rear wheels are attached only by very long wire cables.

Amphibious cars can travel on land and through the water, like boats. They were first developed for military use.

THE AIR CUSHION MAKES IT POSSIBLE TO RIDE ON ANY KIND OF SURFACE

A hovercraft has no wheels. Fans underneath make a cushion of air for it to ride on.

54

Forest-fire fighters use jeeps like this, equipped with hose and big water tanks.

Part of the stage at the Radio City Music Hall in New York is really a truck. The driver lies flat on a little platform underneath and drives the orchestra from the back to the front of the stage.

In India, people sometimes take old, worn-out cars and hitch oxen to them, making them into wagons.

Some very large zoos have automobile trains in which people can ride around the park.

DESIGNING NEW CARS

The designers, engineers, and chemists of the automobile industry never stop working on new ideas. They experiment with new materials, new mechanisms, new paints, new shapes. They work out better ways to build engines, easier ways to steer, more comfortable and safer car bodies.

Artists work out new designs, first on drawing boards, then on huge blackboards, drawing the car from every angle. Next, small models are made of clay. These are studied, changed, and remodeled. When the best of these is selected, a full-sized one is made out of wood so carefully carved and painted that it looks like a real car. This big model is called a mock-up.

ENGINEERS ARE EXPERIMENTING WITH AIR BAGS THAT INFLATE AT THE INSTANT OF COLLISION.

People are more and more concerned with how safe their cars are, so designers have to figure out ways to make the frames stronger and the cars harder to tip over.

Designers have worked out different kinds of safety harnesses; water-filled bumpers that cushion the car if it runs into something; air bags inside the car that inflate around the passengers when there is a crash; steering wheels that collapse out of the way; new kinds of padding; better brakes and tires.

Engineers work to improve car motors so that they will cost less, run more economically, and cause less pollution. The engineers try to improve internal-combustion engines to burn almost all the gasoline, so that no harmful exhaust is put back into the air.

The engineers may try to improve a single part or redesign a whole engine. They experiment with new kinds of engines.

A gas turbine is a jet engine that burns the fuel almost completely and uses the hot exhaust gases to power the engine. It is small and light, with no pistons and no cooling system. A gas turbine has only one-fifth the number of moving parts that a piston engine has, so it needs less maintenance. A gas turbine uses cheaper fuel and gets more miles to the gallon.

Some other experimental engines do not use gasoline at all. Some use steam for power; some use electricity. Some of the earliest cars used these fuels, but they did not have to go as far or as fast as people expect their cars to go now.

ONE KIND OF STEAM CAR USES REFRIGERANT LIQUID TO MAKE STEAM. THE SAME LIQUID IS USED OVER AND OVER.

1. ENGINE HEATS LIQUID

3. STEAM IS COOLED HERE AND RETURNED TO ENGINE AS LIQUID AGAIN

BOILER

2. LIQUID BOILS, MAKING STEAM IN BOILER TO RUN CAR

ROADS AND TRAFFIC

Other engineers work on the problems of making roads safer and getting the always greater numbers of cars to move more smoothly.

They design underpasses and overpasses. They experiment with new road surfaces that grip the tires better. They work out ways to improve highway lighting.

Traffic engineers study traffic. They watch the highways through closed-circuit television, then change or regulate road signals to make traffic flow better. Radio stations broadcast traffic conditions, weather reports, and travelers' warnings. Traffic helicopters watch traffic and broadcast conditions to drivers.

THE CAR FACTORY

A modern automobile factory is as big as a city. It has sheet-metal shops and machine shops, assembly plants, upholstery shops, foundries, docks, restaurants, bus and railway lines. Some plants even have blast furnaces and glass factories.

Automobiles start moving before they are built. All day long in an automobile factory the parts of thousands of cars travel past the workers on assembly lines. Some of the parts move on floor conveyor belts at just the right height for a worker to use his tools most conveniently. Other parts swing from conveyors across the ceiling. At the exact moment a worker is ready to bolt a top onto a car body, it drops into place. Every part is delivered to each workman exactly when he needs it. And when he has done his part of the job, the growing car is carried on to the next man or woman in line.

Each part of the car is assembled in a different section of the factory. In one place, only the engines are put to-

THE FINAL ASSEMBLY LINE IS MORE THAN 800 FEET LONG

THE BODY IS ASSEMBLED AND PAINTED IN A SEPARATE PLACE

THE FRAME AND ENGINE ARE ASSEMBLED

THE WHEELS ARE ATTACHED

gether. As the cylinder block travels on its way it is blasted and sanded and polished. Holes are bored and grooved, sometimes from dozens of directions at once. Parts are fitted in and fastened to it.

In another place a huge machine four stories tall is shaping the body parts of the car out of sheets of steel. These parts move on to be welded together, painted, and upholstered. Many operations in an automobile factory are automated. The work is directed and controlled by computers. No people have to be there at all.

On the final assembly line, which is a single track so long that you cannot see one end from the other, all the parts are put together. Wheels are fastened to the frame; the engine is lowered into place; the steering wheel is set in; the body is dropped on. Workmen tighten and weld and bolt and drive screws and polish as the car goes past them. At the end of the line the car is tested, then driven out of the factory, ready for shipping.

61

HERE ALL THE PARTS ARE PUT TOGETHER, THEN TESTED

THE BODY IS DROPPED ON

THE FRONT END IS ATTACHED

AND EVERYTHING IS TESTED

CAR GAMES

Sometimes you may get tired of just riding, but there are all kinds of games you can play in a car.

You can see how many different state (or country) license plates you can "collect."

Try LICENSE PLATE POKER. Each person in turn takes a passing license plate. The one whose plate makes the best poker hand wins. Count four or three or two numbers or letters of a kind, and numbers in sequence.

THREE OF A KIND

BEATS A RUN OF FOUR

WHICH WINS?

Taking each passing plate in turn, you can play HIGH PLATE WINS. Just add the numbers on each plate, and the highest comes out first. If you have a pencil and pad you can add the totals of several plates, each taking turns.

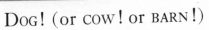

Dog! (or cow! or barn!)
Decide on one of these objects (or any other). The first person who sees it shouts its name. The first to get ten of them wins.

What do you see? is a good game for sharpening your eyes. Look for the out-of-the-ordinary things that you might otherwise ride by without noticing. You'll be surprised at the number of things you've never really seen before, even along a familiar road.

And of course there are a number of games that are fun wherever you are. Twenty questions, What am i?, Ghosts, and Geography, for example, are fine for making long trips seem shorter. The driver, though, needs *his* skill and attention for driving the car safely.

WHEN YOU DRIVE

It may be quite a while before you start driving, but you can be getting ready all the time.

You can begin to notice what makes a good driver.

A good driver is considerate. He is willing to give the right-of-way to another driver or to a boy on a bicycle or to a pedestrian. He wears his seat belt and sees that his passengers do, too.

A good driver does not take chances. He pays strict attention to his driving. He does not drive too fast or pass on curves or weave in and out of traffic. He takes the weather into account.

A good driver has good manners. He does not honk his horn unless there is danger. He does not take more than his share of the road. He tries not to shine his car lights in anyone's eyes. He signals to show other drivers what he is going to do.

AT 20 MILES AN HOUR, IT TAKES 44 FEET TO STOP

AT 50 MILES AN HOUR, IT TAKES 193 FEET TO STOP

A good driver knows his car. He knows how long it takes him to stop when he is going at various speeds. He makes sure that all the mechanical parts of his automobile are in good working order.

A good driver obeys policemen and signal lights and he pays attention to road signs. He knows these are as important to him as lighthouses and buoys are to a ship's captain. The shape of a road sign tells you something even before you can read it. Did you know that—
All eight-sided signs mean STOP?
All round signs mean RAILROAD CROSSING?
All diamond-shaped signs mean CAUTION, SLOW DOWN?
All rectangular signs give information and show local traffic rules?

65

Before you can become a good driver you can be a good passenger.

A good passenger *never* distracts the driver's attention from the road even for a second. He does not point out sights that would make the driver turn his head. He does not create a disturbance in the car.

A good passenger is helpful to the driver. He learns to read road maps. He watches for turnoff signs that the driver might not see.

A good passenger (who is going to become a good driver) learns to know the car. He is helpful in an emergency like changing a tire or putting on skid chains.

When you are ready to start driving, you will take a drivers' education course. Schools all over the United States must provide students with those courses when they are old enough. You will want the course because you know that there is a lot more to driving than steering a car.

BUILD YOUR OWN

You can have a lot of fun with your own car. If you like engines, you might even want to add a motor when you build it (one from an old lawn mower, maybe, or a secondhand electric motor that works on batteries), but you can still use this basic car. However, if you add a motor you MUST have real brakes too. In some places it is against the law to drive a homemade motorized car like this on a public street. So be sure to check the law where you live.

You will need:

A box.
1 board, 14 inches wide, 60 inches long, and about 1¼ inches thick. (If you prefer, you can nail two narrower ones together like this.)

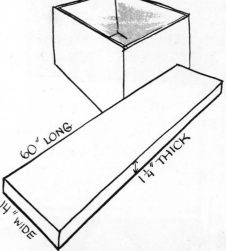

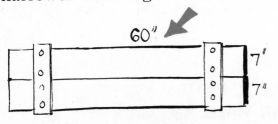

60" 7" 7"

CARRIAGE WHEELS AND AXLES

35 MM FILM SPOOL

NAILS

PULLEYS

U-BOLTS

WASHERS

CARRIAGE BOLT

3 YARDS OF WIRE ROPE

2 boards, 4 inches wide, 20 inches long, and about 1¼ inches thick.
2 sticks, each 2 inches square, one 14 inches long, one 24 inches long.
4 baby carriage wheels about 12 inches across.
2 metal axles. (Maybe you can find an old baby carriage, from which you can get both wheels and axles. Otherwise you can buy them at a carriage repair shop.)
A 35-mm film spool for a steering wheel. (You can get this at a camera store.)
4 ¼-inch U-bolts.
1 ½-inch x 4-inch carriage bolt.
A dozen or so large washers.
4 small clothesline pulleys.
3 yards of ¼-inch wire rope.
2-inch common nails.

Nail one of the 4-inch boards across the long board like this. Fix the axle, with wheels attached, to the board like this, with two of the U-bolts.

68

BOTTOM VIEW OF
REAR WHEEL ASSEMBLY

Fix the other set of wheels and axle to the second narrow board. Then, using the washers and the carriage bolt like this, fasten the whole assembly to the long board. These are the front wheels and they steer. The rear wheels push.

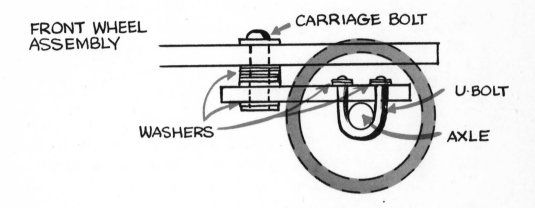

FRONT WHEEL
ASSEMBLY

CARRIAGE BOLT

WASHERS

U·BOLT

AXLE

Now nail the steering wheel in place with the two square sticks, like this.

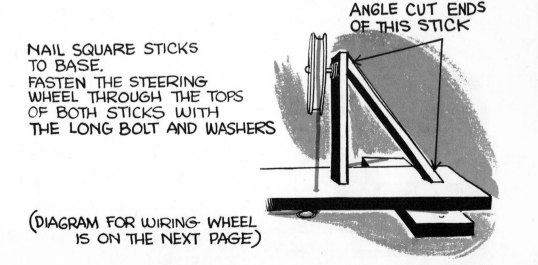

ANGLE CUT ENDS
OF THIS STICK

NAIL SQUARE STICKS
TO BASE.
FASTEN THE STEERING
WHEEL THROUGH THE TOPS
OF BOTH STICKS WITH
THE LONG BOLT AND WASHERS

(DIAGRAM FOR WIRING WHEEL
IS ON THE NEXT PAGE)

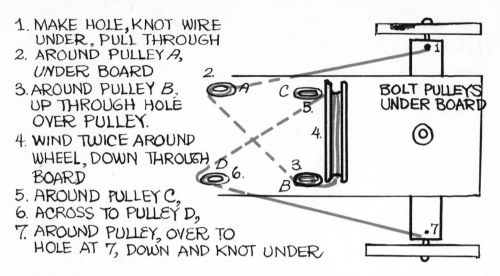

1. MAKE HOLE, KNOT WIRE UNDER, PULL THROUGH
2. AROUND PULLEY A, UNDER BOARD
3. AROUND PULLEY B, UP THROUGH HOLE OVER PULLEY.
4. WIND TWICE AROUND WHEEL, DOWN THROUGH BOARD
5. AROUND PULLEY C,
6. ACROSS TO PULLEY D,
7. AROUND PULLEY, OVER TO HOLE AT 7, DOWN AND KNOT UNDER

BOLT PULLEYS UNDER BOARD

Following the diagram, carefully rig the wire rope so it connects the steering wheel to the front wheel section.

Now place your box, open end up, so it is just the right distance from the steering wheel to be a comfortable backrest. It can hold freight or another passenger.

From here on, you can make your car as fancy as you please. But be sure you have a good mechanic check your car for safety before you use it.

INDEX

71